H IS FOR HARRY

H IS FOR HARRY

POEMS

SUSAN SINK

NORTH STAR PRESS OF ST. CLOUD, INC.

St. Cloud, Minnesota

ISBN: 978-1-68201-018-1

FIRST EDITION: MARCH 2016

PRINTED IN THE UNITED STATES OF AMERICA.

PUBLISHED BY

NORTH STAR PRESS

P.O. BOX 451

ST. CLOUD, MN 56302

www.northstarpress.com

For my mother, Nancy Sink,
who taught me every letter
and showed me the world they made.

TABLE OF CONTENTS

PARK SLOPE, BROOKLYN, 1990

My friend said you should never
sleep in the room where you worked.
I could only afford a single room,
but I found one split by pocket doors.

I wrote at the one table in the place,
and slept in the interior dark, my head
against the air shaft of the former tenement.
The day's poems no longer haunted my dreams.

But through the shaft came squeaks of love
and angry shouts from the second floor,
the homeless man's wheezing in the stairwell,
the aggressive buses and sirens of ambulances.

I gave up and slid the doors into the walls,
let in the streetlight and defiant click of after-hour stilettos,
rode the wake of snowplows and street sweepers,
awakened to bagpipes leading a parade down Seventh.

My friend, an accountant, closed the door
on numbers and clients, and slept in peace.
But my work was poetry, night music,
which no door could keep out, the very stuff of dreams.

PRECIOUS THINGS

My sister brought home precious things and our mother made her take them back. When she was four she went to a yard sale and for a nickel bought a gold French horn in a velvet-lined box. I had never seen anything so beautiful. I couldn't believe she thought she could own such a thing. Our mother said it was worth more than a nickel and was for an adult or older child who could play it. My sister tried to take it back, but the woman at the garage sale wanted her to have it. I loved that horn and that velvet-lined box, though none of us could make it play.

When she was seven, my sister brought home a dead bird she found on the sidewalk on her way from school. When she walked in the door, cradling the bird to her cheek, our mother screamed. My sister dropped the bird and cried. The bird was beautiful, but it probably had parasites. When they calmed down, my mother got a shoebox and they buried the beautiful thing in the backyard.

When she was ten, my sister brought home a brand new couch that Mrs. L. had put at the curb. Our mother saw her and her friends carrying it past the kitchen window to furnish our makeshift clubhouse. She made them take it back to the curb, explaining that it was left there for poor people who didn't have a couch in their house, not for clubhouses. It was a sofa bed. It was very heavy. Mrs. L. had something called "agoraphobia." She didn't come outside and she was afraid of germs. When she offered you a box of tissues, she always offered you the second one, so you wouldn't get the dust on the top tissue.

For my sister, the world is full of precious things.

TRAVELING ABROAD, DURING THE RAIN,
I LONG FOR A JAPANESE NOVEL

I wish I had a lovely Japanese novel here,
but I have traveled light as a pilgrim. Still,
I have them by heart, have lived them page by page:
chased the fireflies down the banks,
swept locust shells from the corners
of the four-*tatami* attic room. I've lit the lanterns
and let the glow wake me and put me out,
arranged a single orchid in a gourd and called it spring,
given that glance meant not to say too much,
accompanied by the briefest sliver of shoulder blade
in the hopes of a match, all the while
preferring to remain alone and fluttering
like a gingko's yellow, melancholy leaves.

Keep the tales of warriors and harsh beauty,
the blood and swords, tattoo and blunt words.
Give me the puppet theater of Osaka, the monks
sweeping the courtyard, the old ones heading out
on pilgrimage with a proverb inscribed on the brim
of a woven hat. Give me the *haiku* they will write!
Leave behind the efficient widowed daughter
who has done her best to make a go, with typing
and telephones, in the offices of Tokyo.
Let the high speed train make only one stop,
at a station nestled in snow banks near the inn,
and to the hot spring bath the hero will clip clop
in his *geta*, wrapped in white towels.
Let me hear once only the sad song of the *samisen*
expertly played. Let me smell on her handkerchief
the scent of powder. Let me see the pines and know
their whisper even at a distance, through the window.

THE WORLD

Where am I going to go? Father Patrick asks,
dressed like this? He spreads his arms
to demonstrate his sandal-clad feet,
the drape of robe cinched by a leather belt.
To a movie? Like this? To a poetry reading?

Why not? I want to ask. I've seen him dressed
quite casually, on his way from the Jewel
with a bag of groceries slung over his arm.
The magazines at the checkout stand, my God!
he exclaims to the Oblates. *How can you live
out there, so assaulted every hour of every day?*

Still, I know, at six each morning he takes advantage
of the slim hour between psalms to slip
to the basement treadmill or bike.
There he rides in place and slides the dial
ever so slightly from its notch on Beethoven
to NPR and the news. He stares at the brick wall -
and catches up on the voices of the world.

Then he showers, tightens his belt,
and returns to silence and to prayer.

4

SONG FOR THE GREEN SEASON

after Elizabeth Bishop

The cock whose clock is off
   crows loudly for light
two hours before the day
   complies, and not to be outdone
     every other rooster replies.

What dark alarm, the butterflies beating to no effect.

I wake to the insistent tick
   of the clock I've thrust
in the bedside drawer,
   Poe's heart telling me
to face it, face it.

   Three o'clock to five I lie
awake until white light precedes
   the pink splash of sun
     in the village pot.

The birds get up
   for breakfast and scold
the cocks their ruckus.

The cocks give over their watch and sleep.

The termites are so sated with decay
   they need not resort to furniture;
the phosphorescent beetles feed
   on fallen fruit.

The ants set sail on green leaves,
   an armada of gardeners
     on the mossy path.

Where is the *I* in this storm
  of order and disorder?

The fetid abundance of this green season,
  wounded fruit, starched wings,
walk me into the dailiness
  of everlasting life.

MEDITATION FOR A CENTURY JUST BEGUN

Bow down five times a day, or seven.
Sing the psalms in an unlit sanctuary.
Sit in any pose and stare at the wall.
Burn incense, burn a candle, burn a sacrifice.

The centuries are calling your name.

What language do you speak?
Translate the word of life into a tongue
Unspeakable. How would you answer then?

And if God said to you: leave your family, right now,
And if God said to you: say what I will say
And the world will listen, and if God said to you:
Love this man, offer your son, do it for me,

Would you argue? Would you take up arms?
Beat them into ploughshares and sow seeds
Altered to bear three times the normal yield?
Would you feed them or would you feed
The Word of God in a strange land, one untouched
Yet, and how would it sound in their ears?
How would it sound in their hunger?

What would you see there, your own wealth
You never before considered, or something new,
Humility you knew as an idea but which now
Strikes you dumb? Do something small
And then something smaller and then
The smallest thing, a gesture, very slight.
Consider whether it's brave. And if these three
Movements make an action, and if it helps
You feel alive, or names you love, or opens
Your heart, your ears, any window, any door—

Go to the beginning and listen again. Listen hard.

THE STORY OF MY NAME

My mother told me I was named after a little girl named Susan who was my father's first fare every day when he drove a cab. His father had a combination junkyard and cab company in South Jersey in the fifties and sixties.

My father drove the cab to put himself through college at the Rutgers campus in Camden. Every morning he would pick up Susan and her mother and drop Susan off at school.

In my imagination, Susan was a character from a Tasha Tudor illustrated book. She wore a wool coat and had a fur muff to keep her hands warm. She was dainty and had dark, curly hair and dark eyes. She was a little girl my father would love so much that later he would name his firstborn after her.

My mother later told me that Susan was a disabled child. She went to a special school and that is why she needed to ride in a taxi each morning. This made me love my father even more.

When I asked my father about this story, he said he did remember driving a woman and her daughter to school, but he didn't think the girl's name was Susan.

THE SADNESS OF POETRY

He was from Nicaragua and loved the sadness of poetry.
He could recite the sonnets of Pablo Neruda
and poems by Gabriela Mistral and Antonio Machado
that translated the moonlight and scent of flowers into aching love.

He worried about the power of poetry and its intent,
where it could lead you and where it could leave you.
He worried that his love of poetry was a dangerous one,
like his love of the tango, which he had nurtured for years,

until he could no longer stand the excruciating sadness.
One day he had finally freed himself of the tango,
tossing out a shelf of recordings, his entire collection.
He thought he had averted disaster, was free and clear.

Now he realized poetry had the same hold on him.
What happiness could come from it? Could it lead you
out of your pain and suffering, not deeper into it?
Could it ever be made of the very stuff of happiness?

COLLAPSE

It was a year of collapsing. The towers were only first.

I should have known, because I kept calling you
and you didn't come home:

But there are people jumping from the windows.

But there are people waiting at the hospitals, and no casualties arriving.

I fear they are all, terribly, dead.

We got lost three times that year, twice when snow obscured the path,
and once in the desert.

All three times we pretended what we saw were trails,
or exclaimed at familiar landmarks that turned unfamiliar.

You climbed to the top of hills to scout our way, and returned
shaking your head:

I can't see any way out.
I can't see anything. I don't know the way.

H IS FOR HARRY

I was not yet three when I learned to read
letter by letter, with my mother,
using comic strips from the newspaper.
The first one taught me the letter *h*.
H makes the sound of *huh*.
Huh-huh-huh-Harry. The strip
had a picture of Harry running.
His breathing was the letter *h*: *huh-huh-huh*.
When Harry was tired he sat on a chair.
The chair was the shape of the letter *h*.
Huh-huh-huh-Harry. Huh-huh-huh-hot.
A letter *h* to sit on, and letter *h* your breath.
My mother and I said it together:
Huh-huh-huh-hat. Huh-huh-huh-hop.
Huh-huh-happy. Huh-huh-hug.
And then it was mine, to find in books
and on signs and in the kitchen chair: the letter *h*.

BABYSITTING

I sat in the passenger seat of the Camaro
while Mr. Hansen drove me home in silence.
I'd spent four Friday-night hours in his home,
eating the potato chips and ice cream,
browsing the bookshelves, reading
Helter Skelter and the latest critique
of the Warren Commission Report.
I wanted to ask him about Charles Manson
and whether Lee Harvey Oswald acted alone.

Mr. Hansen was the high school tennis coach,
taught honor's algebra, where I sat in my assigned seat
in the back and struggled. But that was later.
In junior high I watched his daughter, Julie,
who liked to play *Sorry!* and eat Peeps at Easter
and went to bed without an argument.

TOUGH GIRLS

In high school our friend Hildy suddenly went quiet. Stealthy. We never saw her change her clothes for gym—she somehow made herself disappear and reappear. When she ate her lunch, she kept the food in her lunch bag and moved it to her mouth without us seeing what she ate. She stopped going out with us. She quit the tennis team. I knew something was going on in her house. I saw the way she watched her older brother in the cafeteria.

One day on our way to English class, this tough black girl named Lisa was walking in front of us. A small black boy came running up to her, agitated, talking fast. Without breaking stride, Lisa punched him. He flew up against the wall and, like a cartoon, slid down, stunned. You could almost see the stars spinning over his head. Hildy turned to me, beaming—*Did you see that? Did you SEE that?!*

Lisa was in our philosophy class. She sat in back with a stoner named Chris. They asked a lot of questions. Hildy and I sat in front. After that day in the hall, Hildy talked to Lisa somehow. Every time we passed in the hall she yelled out, *Hey, Hildy!* Hildy nodded and smiled in return, the smallest, inscrutable smile.

HIGH PLACES

At fifteen, I read an allegory
about a girl who climbed a mountain,
beset by Pride and assaults of Loneliness.
She was crippled, but assisted by Suffering and Sorrow.

At the top, she asked to be bound to an altar
so a savior could pull the many-tendrilled weed
of Human Love tightly wound around her heart.
It almost killed her to have it removed.

After this, she was no longer herself,
but joined the creatures of the allegory,
her new name a phrase, her legs those of a deer.
Everything was Grace and Glory and Joy and Peace.

I cried and cried, reading this book,
because I was fifteen and full of desire.

I'LL TAKE YOU HOME AGAIN

When Johnny Cash sings to Kathleen
that simple folk song of longing for Ireland,
and promises to take her home again,
it becomes a hymn in a backwoods church,
and Ireland becomes heaven, Kathleen dead,
promises empty and nothing left but regret.

When Johnny Cash mournfully croons the line:
and tears bedim your loving eyes,
it is a Christian mother who cries
because her son has gone astray, to drink,
even so far as prison, some motherless place,
and the only one who can help is Jesus.

And then by song's end it is Jesus at last
promising to take Johnny, all us poor sinners,
to where your heart will feel no pain
and where the fields are lush and green,
to take us all home again.

MAGI

On an oak hutch wrestled from the rectory
Father Patrick's Spode Blue china was offered up
For Sale. Each day he prayed it would not sell
before he prayed for the desire to see it sold.

He thought of the click of cup on saucer
and the way the lip registers the sensation
of porcelain edge and sweet hot tea.
He thought of the good food the sale would provide.

Short and squat and unrefined, the buyer
was a shop teacher in the Projects,
wanted the china for his wife, their anniversary,
and offered to build an altar in exchange.

The Jehovah's Witness kids from Cabrini Green
said: *This better not be no table for a church*
but turned and lathed for the credits
the recycled pews into pillars and table top.

At the start of Mass, Patrick kisses the linen,
and the paten is delicate as porcelain in his hands,
daily offering up the unbroken bread,
raising the heavy chalice with its sweet red wine.

Then there are the days when the cloth
is put away and the altar stands fine-grained,
incense deep in its grooves, and promises
to hold the world, all its suffering and all its gifts.

ATLANTIC

How little we knew, about oceans, about ourselves,
when we lingered in the jellyfish minefield of the Atlantic,
those raft-stuffed waves we rode like cowboys,
thinking cowboys were figments of fifties matinees.
Ashore we kept between South Jersey's sludge pipes
and clumped the boardwalk's noisy, creosote strip.

Each year commerce encroached a little farther
and demanded our salt water dollars; Christ stood at the door
and knocked in the souvenir splendor of Wildwood,
and *Playboy* silhouettes silk-screened the T-shirts we bought
to commemorate our late-seventies, merry-go-round visits.

What did we know? Even those years we abandoned
the neon boardwalk for Cape May's aviary attractions.
Our father haunted the pavilion to hear the barbershop quartets
at appointed intervals, and the unapproachable Victorians
turned their parlored faces to us,

                                telling us to get back inland
to the immigrant bay, the cottage where priests visited Mrs. Mohr
like the stations, and we luxuriated in outdoor showers
and tri-fold "chaise lounge" beds. Sand puddled the concrete
and braided girls named Eileen and Colleen arrived after midnight
and left after breakfast, so we had Michael, that archangel surfer
to ourselves, and the snail-puckered shore of the bay.

What did we know? What did we ever know
of childhood, of youth, of love, with its
octopus of arms, with its jellyfish sting on our hearts?
When did we realize it was America all along,
loving us and killing us every hour?

CONEY ISAND

You, sister, were the only one
willing to ride with me
on the Ferris wheel
unlike any other;
the cars lurching on
an inside track
as the wide wheel,
haltingly,
turned us around.

DECEMBER, JANUARY, FEBRUARY

Father Patrick wakes every dark morning
to the daily alarm of the novice
down the hall making a fire in his wood stove:
the *crumple crumple crumple crunch* of paper,
then the lighter, *click, click, click* . . .

Every day, over and over again
until the banked stove catches and warms.

The older monk can see his breath,
and the patience of the novice tries
his own. The creaturely comfort
of the curled cat at the foot of his bed
masks the turmoil of his undisciplined head.
He pats the cat and waits. He eyes his books.

After all these years, as parish priest
and now as monk, contemplating
book by book and psalm by psalm
the world and its poetry, the world beyond
and Christ's love love love love love.

Crumple, crumple, crumple, crunch,
the novice nudges the news beneath
the kindling and tries again, *click, click,*
click, and now his lungs heave
to blow, blow, bellow to life the fire.

POLAND

for Adam Zagajewski

Whenever I pass on the highway
a small Midwestern town,
say St. Joseph, Minnesota, with the dome
of its nineteenth-century monastery,
the suggestion of a town above the trees,
and farms to the highway, I think of Poland
which I've never seen, a Poland
I suspect no longer exists even in tatters,
like this small town visible from the highway.

I imagine Poland now as beautiful ruins
and long white stone faces of the Virgin
and cold concrete hotels with bad carpeting
and hard beds and an antiseptic smell.
I imagine it as the hive of apartments
in Kieslowski's *Decalogue*, where ordinary
failures break every commandment.

I may never get to Poland, but Poland
does and does not exist. I know snow
and dark and streetlights, and church towers
behind trees, and a hill with a rolled haystack
at dusk. Already at that monastery
where there once lived twelve hundred nuns
there are no more than eighty at prayer.
I have heard them singing the psalms
in their dimly lit, carpeted chapel, voices
like the rubbed rims of crystal glasses.

RILKE AND THE PARROTS

Rilke, in a dry spell, walks the bicycle path
in Long Beach, California, near his patron's estate.

He is trying to see deeply into things. He is listening
for what the world of America will tell him.

His next great sequence is somewhere here
hidden in his heart, in the air, in another lovesick panic.

He's fled the Continent to escape her, the charismatic
lover dancing in and out of his dreams,

into the healing arms of a wealthy broker couple
who love poetry and Europeans, and have offered

the kind of shelter necessary for visits from angels.
But now he finds the angst dissipating; language escapes him.

Ahead, a movie shoot encamps the parking lot.
He is tempted by fame, but close up he finds it banal.

It is just a jogging scene for a t.v. show set in Miami.
The extras reset, and everyone stares, trying not to expect too much.

Time for Rilke to turn back. There is nothing here.
The cruise ship idles alongside the white dome

where Howard Hughes once moored his sea plane.
Spruce Goose, Rilke intones, conjuring Hughes's uncut fingernails.

Americans love their eccentrics, but what he's found
is this place is too crowded for epiphany. Even the sunset is obstructed

by oil derricks and the cranes of the port. The sea all
near-dusk phosphorescence is held back by a breakwall.

And now the last exotic harangue. It is time for the parrots,
and here they come, a flock of escaped pets sweeping down Ocean Blvd.

Arraying themselves in a palm tree, pretending chaos, they chatter
like Styrofoam or the squeaky wheels of Friars's tiny cars.

What a racket! is all Rilke can think to think.
Ruined, ruined, my mind. It's a wrap, the walk, this coast.

He came here to live in the style to which he'd grown
to expect poetry, the creature comforts taken care of.

He came here because he is urban, really, not ever inspired
by the vast spaces, any scene without a path running through it.

New York is too cold, and Paris too poor, and London, well,
they bombed it to pieces and put up a blue plaque in its memory.

But any day now there will be notices from the art colonies,
and finally some place to go, appropriate, hopefully the one

where the children died tragically and their paintings,
larger than life, still grace the dining room.

DESERT SESTINA

I feel at home in Joshua Tree's desert.
There's peace in the vast emptiness,
the illusion that you could never get lost
because you can see so far, and sounds carry
over desert like they carry over water,
alerting others to your presence on or off the trail.

Have you ever noticed how two women on a trail
will talk and talk, never running empty,
but couples are more quiet? In the desert
they stop briefly to share a bottle of water
as if time together allows them to be at a loss
for words, or many ways to show they care.

I pay attention to these things now; I care
what brought these people to the desert,
and wonder if it makes them feel full or empty,
the barren rock beneath a sky the color of water.
I know it's hard for anyone to stay on the trail
and in the world, as in the desert, easy to get lost.

Two years ago my husband and I got lost
following a wash we mistook for the trail.
Four hours we walked in the dark in the desert,
each ridge we climbed showing us more emptiness.
My husband was worried. He tried to take care
of me. I told him it was warm and we had water.

Finally we saw the lights of the highway, like water,
an oasis of cars, and we walked toward it, far from any trail.
I felt oddly peaceful in sight of town. I didn't care
how far we had to walk through the emptiness.
I didn't know that my husband was already lost.
Finally, we reached a medical center, nearly deserted.

It would be less than three months before he would desert
me and our marriage, leave me like a fish out of water,
flopping. I was left to find my way, build a new trail
out of my grief over so large a loss.
Watching him go down so fast, that he didn't care
enough to try, left a deep, vast emptiness.

I revisit that loss, working it out in the desert.
I stay on the trail and carry plenty of water.
I know in the big emptiness there's also clarity, bedrock.

COVERING GROUND

Weekdays I went down into the tunnels,
rumbled under the dark river, counted bright stops,
emerged into the palace of Grand Central
and rose to the twenty-fourth floor, where I looked down
the long boulevard of Park Avenue
with its cabs, trees strung with lights,
and VIP flags of the Waldorf Astoria,
to the west a view of Rockefeller's tower.

On Saturdays I'd ride. Neither high nor low,
I stayed on the ground. I went places.

To my right
the broad boulevard broken by stoplights,
impediments that sharpened the view,
women skirted and scarved pushing strollers,
Hasidic men in scholarly dispute, chess players,
babushkas on benches taking a load off.
People lived in houses here.

All the way to Coney Island
and the hollowed, rusted rides,
the freak show I never entered,
the aquarium under renovation.
I ate hand pies hawked by Puerto Ricans
on the pier, watched the men drop cages
baited with raw chicken and pull up crabs.
Cerveza fria sold from sagging grocery bags
dripping ice melt as the men trudged
drunkenly through the sand to make a buck.

There were children looking over the rail
and out at the sea who grew up this way.

To my left
down the street where Marianne Moore
lived in a prim, satisfactory four-flat,
over Hart Crane's bridge into the city,
the stately, inflexible park of City Hall,
the banking industry of Canal Street,
banners of SoHo, six miles of books,
cheap socks of Chelsea, my Midtown, now quiet,
over through diamonds or fashion or flowers,
right up some far western avenue and back
to the Park. I covered as much of the earth
as I could cover block by block.

One night when I still lived in Westchester
I left my bike at the Pelham station overnight
and returned to find it stripped, all wires gone,
and hacked at with some blunt instrument.
Somehow the lock kept its promise.
I carried the torso two blocks to the bike shop
where almost everything was replaced.

I shipped that scarred machine, my steed,
to California and rode it again, hard,
up the hills and deep into the Eucalyptus forest,
over all the burnt hills of Silicon Valley,
to every movie theater and bookstore within reach.

After those years of lonely, forced beauty,
I sold it for twenty bucks, bought a car,
and moved to Chicago. My parents thought
I was growing up at last, my first new car.

And maybe I was. I know I never saw as much
of the world from that car as from my bicycle,
which took me farther than I ever expected,
from sea to shining sea.

MOUNT RAINIER

What you see from Seattle is not what it is, ice octopus.
The glaciers look harmless through the free telescope.

What it is, volcano, is clear from the air. You make out the crater
beneath all that snow and know someday it will blow.

From Seward Park it looks like a backdrop,
and the camera doesn't capture its vague beauty.

Are we on the mountain yet? a child asks from the backseat.
Yes, he is told, but he just sees a road with trees
and can't understand the long drive to the parking lot,
to the snow and the visitor's center.

I think of Whitman and wonder: *What is a mountain?*
I look under my bootsoles for an answer, and the gray-haired Whitman says:

"I think it is a tower of Babel, taunting us with our distance from the heavens,
        confounding us at the top.
Or it is a photographer's rig, the green draped over his stooped shoulders
and lens as he gazes at us.
Or else it is the root of mathematics by which we make distance triangulate, a
        number.
Perhaps it is a chess piece, advanced by God to check, a strike against the
poor defense of pawns aligned along the coast.

And now it seems a foreshadowing of all we cannot know—
the center of the earth rising to the sky,
the north pushed south, the south pressing north,
always something just over the next peak, out of reach,
a world beyond breath, making us fish in the sea of earth.

And it seems to me we are fish of the earth, thinking all the time we are
angels, forgetting snow burns like fire, its reflection can blind us.
It is the mountain that tells us the infinite is not the illusion, the grand sky not
ours, for we are wrapped in a fragile glass bowl of air."

HARVESTING THE STONE

In spring, when the snow finally melted,
before the potatoes and earliest peas were planted,
we saw the stones that had heaved upward,
unearthed themselves, littering the field.

We had a week off school then, to pick rock,
the boys and me groaning under the largest ones,
the younger kids fitting small hands to stones,
rattling them onto the trailer bed.

The tractor growled and inched forward,
and Dad looked back from the seat, urging us.
If we missed one and later a blade got broke,
we knew how that repair would cost us all.

The biggest stones we'd lever into the bucket
and dad would hoist them out one by one.
It was stones like those that built the church
and the grotto to the Blessed Mother.

That was back in 1856. My grandfather made
his contribution, stones like loaves of bread,
an offering from the land itself. Built of stones
that grew each year. The first crop. First harvest.

MILOSZ AND THE PARROTS

There is a woman climbing stairs.
She ascends and descends.
The stairs are red concrete and lead
from bluff to beach, beach to bluff.
Feral cats watch from a plastic igloo
tucked into scrub that tenuously holds
the hillside. The sun glints off
aluminum food trays, is absorbed
into the gray green of sand and vegetation.

A man turns and takes the steps two by two.
His body does not alter as he runs,
the roundness of biceps, calves, ass,
his feet cast in some space-age material.

The woman does not look defeated.
She looks forty-five and set to a task.
The task does not give her pleasure;
her body is strong and simply works.

On the beach someone has walked into the sand:
GOD LOVES YOU in large letters.
It can only be read from the bluff.
Now a man arrives with his close-cut beard
and save-the-earth T-shirt and designer shorts
and stomps in an alternate message:
DOG LOVES YOU. His zeal
is astonishing. His outrage. His claim.
How will he save the earth like that?

When the exotic parrots come in a flock
down the boulevard they stay high.
We hardly believe in them. The cats look up
because they cannot do otherwise.
The woman shields her eyes and turns to the noise.
Her arm is an empty wing, her brow a bright crest.

LOFT

His kisses were bruises. I made him stop. The windows were mirrors, like watching a performance of ourselves. I said I should go, but he convinced me to stay and read poetry and sleep. We retreated into the dark cavern of good taste, his abstract paintings on their easels, paint puddled on the floor.

In the morning when I saw the bruises I wondered how I'd brave the subway home.

Then I saw the rising sun light up the cornices and gargoyles across the avenue. That exquisite row of buildings, that place and time unlike any other. It had the loss of the Great Wars in it. It had the hopes of the New World. It had the grime of Civilization.

What price, that view. What beauty. What pain, that beauty.

THE STORY OF MY NAME

I married twice but kept my "maiden name." My given name. My birth name.

I playfully considered changing it when I first married. My name would have been Susan Hart. I Googled the name years later and discovered there was a porn star named Susan Hart who lived in Los Angeles, where I was also living. We would not only have shared a name but also a birthdate: month, day, and year.

As an art project before we got married, I made a list of all the combinations joining my name, Sink, with my husband's name, Hart, to find a suitable hybrid we could use. Our favorite was Shark.

My sister and her children always addressed cards and letters to me as Mrs. Susan Hart. This stopped bothering me when my niece sent a letter addressed to Mrs. Susan Heart.

BRINGING THE BODY DOWN

I

The Chinook hovers in the light atmosphere,
blades struggling to keep the heavy-bellied craft
afloat and off the berg of Mount Rainier.
Search and rescue where the bright blue sky
exposes one body in bright orange gear
near the collapsed cave of snow, and there,
yellow as a chalk outline, in the crevasse,
the second woman where she lay. Search, not rescue.
The pilot wheels round with a change in mission,
while from the southwest a new system rolls in.
The team hurries and with precision hooks
the litter to the Chinook and spools the wire aboard.

One left in the crevasse that will cradle her
until the team on foot ascends the following day.
No rush now, both dead on the rock. Search,
not rescue. Onboard the men drown in icy air
and the litter crackles under the tarpaulin
tucked to shield them from that frozen face,
the nightmare's china-blue face of the girl,
lids closed and lashes frosted, hair matted
with ice and snow to her hood. Down, down,
the farms with cattle lowing, Seattle's needle,
the green promise of June. School's out.

2

The one who fell and survived, screwed
himself to the ice in dark wind and awaited dawn,
shudders at blackened fingers and toes. His face
doesn't move beneath the light dressing, the skin
its own entity, expressions of grief, of relief, denied
all but his eyes, which reveal exhaustion and panic.

Alle sind tot, he thinks. *Aber wie?*
How can it happen in America? So close to the city?
He's been to the Alps, Tyrolean heights, Thailand,
and Mount Fuji and Everest, and this suburban mountain
did them in? So much equipment he'd laughed,
yes, his voice had made such a sound, at America.
Vorsicht ist besser als Nachsicht.

Four days to the summit, from Liberty Cap,
where a storm the newspaper called "a giant mousetrap"
caught them and one by one their survivor plans
collapsed in the wind, in stumbling unseeing
sheer drops, until he screwed himself to the slope
and waited through the dark night. He shivers now—
when if ever will he cease to hear the howl
of wind and return to thoughts of the women above,
hoping they're safe in that assault of snow
and wind, concentrating his heat inward.
America, how could I have underestimated you?

3

Olympus had no god of snow, so we were charged
to name him, but when we reached this mountain
our one true God had overtaken all the others
and left us to make monsters instead. With careful
plans and gear we try to conquer them.

The rangers walk onto the mountain, loaded
with ropes, ice-axes, their strong calves
churning above the gaiters and boot-tops,
packs light for the one-day round-trip trek.
Flags wave bright blazes behind them,
where they've planted a trail to follow down
after they've dragged the yellow body,
right-sided from the icy fault line out
onto the shining face of the mountain.

Already below, tourists like ants crawl
the plain by the visitor center, unprepared
in sea-level sandals and socks, no glasses or gloves,
forgetting snow is cold enough to burn,
bright enough to sear vision from their eyes.
But weather will not catch them unaware,
the way it did these climbers summiting.

4

In the visitor center we use the telescope
to focus on the crew's descent,
small mammals in a world of white.
Solidly mounted to the walls is the
pre-history of the mountain, an exhibit
my friend and her kids look blankly on:
the world God made is not so old, they scoff;
these are the myths of secular civilization.

Would God pluck them from the mountain top,
these children too squeamish for the outhouse?
They would not have the hubris to ascend,
well-versed in the lessons of Babel,
Jonah swallowed whole by a whale a truer tale
than the fossil evidence and mastodon bones.

Still, they seem to know God doesn't ever pluck;
God answers mother-prayers with no;
His lessons are obscure, and sometimes
He punishes. Wrack and ruin. Search and rescue.
The children pray that night, for the blue-faced
girls and boy, and the one lying in a bed alive,
that they may someday see God's glory in the skies.

A GIRL

I went camping in the Sierras, three mothers with young children and me, newly single. One woman brought along her babysitter. Her name was Ng Oo. She was from Burma.

We swam in Doris Lake. She told me about her family's life. Her job had been to keep the brazier going, the glow of a single piece of coal where the family cooked food. She missed her brother.

She was slight and her voice was soft. She wore a large, plastic brace like a corset, because she had broken her back on a hike. She'd remove the brace, slip into the water, and swim.

She was off to Humboldt State in the fall. My e-mail to her was returned. I gave one of my students her name when he transferred to Humboldt State. Ng Oo. Find her, I said.

AFTER *THE ENTRY OF CHRIST INTO CHICAGO IN 1976* BY ROGER BROWN

In 1976 Christ entered Chicago
on a flatbed truck. People lined the street,
joined in a paper doll row, and many more
occupied offices, one to each yellow pane
of Prudential, Hancock, Sears. The bridge was raised
over the river, but no matter, because Christ crossed
farther west and made his way to the platform
where the cardinal, two country western singers,
and a committee of politicians awaited him.

Those who were dancing continued to dance.
Those who were eating raised forks to their mouths.
Those who were working continued as always with here and there
one or two pressing faces against windows—
though for the sunset alone, the city itself,
or with some shiver of Christ's entrance
on their minds, we don't know.

By 1978, Christ had made his way to the outskirts of Chicago,
moving south, unaffiliated with cardinals or congressmen
or a particular style of music. Word of his work,
even some miracles, healings, localized prophecy,
did not make the papers. The sun set that day
and though nothing had changed, everything had changed.
Christ entered the town of Park Forest through the telephone wires.

Those in school passed their papers forward, entered *here*
or *present* in the ledger. Those fathers on trains
pulled into I.C. stations in the city, less than an hour by express.
Here and there a television set caught his entry; a man nailing siding
to a garage inexplicably stirred. A mother in her sickbed and empty,
dialed the number at the bottom of the television screen, and it was a woman's
voice that answered and with welcome, hard invitation, opened an invisible door.

AFTER VESPERS, SATURDAY

In front six monks hunker down
In the oak envelopes of pews
Embroidered with carved cloverleaf,
Ear to ear with God.
They sit masked by the white tent
Of hoods, meditating or nodding
This brief hour of darkness and candlelight
Between vespers and the meal, this slight
Respite before the last duty of day, and sleep.
The harpsichord stands in its case, slim posture
At the ready behind the bench, poised for
Tomorrow's noisy public—but not so the brothers,
Who hunch, having just left one week of hours
For the next, a server blessed, a server charged to bless,
A reader who has been silent opening his mouth to song.
No easy business, this work of silence.
They make a distinction in this vocation:
Not to pray for the work but to work for the prayer.
So here, after the day's work, to sit present for peace,
Wherever they are in their separate lives, together,
To wait in joyful hope for the coming—
The new bells chime six o'clock unassisted,
Each one as it has been named and blessed:
Benedict, Geoffrey, Hildegard, Benedict—
Without a word they rise to supper,
A new week turning, Ordinary Time.

OH HUMMINGBIRD!

How could you know as you flew
your vast migratory path, today
I'd hang this basket of fuchsia?

I can't imagine you loitering
through fickle April into early May
with the big, hardy birds of early spring.

Or are you like the bluebottles,
made of heat and brightness, conjured
into being from a small crease in the oak,

called forth by my hopeful act,
the fuchsia's Chinese lanterns
full of sweetness, little ringing bells?

This basket began in a hothouse in February,
just as you forsook the white sand
and expanse of overwhelming blue.

Just wait! Be still! In a month the exotic lilies
will open their nectar mouths and speak
in your native tongue, reminding you of home.

HOPE

When my husband left, I set up shop at the dining room table. It looked out over the whole apartment and to the balcony. That was my domain.

He was a vegetarian who ate fish. I let all the fish in the freezer turn into a single block of ice. I ate red meat and spinach and not much else.

There was a neglected hanging plant on the balcony and the day after he left a pigeon nested there.

One day I locked my car in the garage and couldn't get it out.

I smashed some expensive pottery he gave me in the alley.

Then one day I looked up and realized it wasn't a pigeon nesting on my balcony. It was a dove.

PACIFIC

I'm looking for a message from the sea, and yet
this place, epic and brooding, Jeffers' stiff drink, turns only
the indifference of granite, the illusion of a precarious stack,
rock on rock, the fissures ancient. What eyes me here
is the circle hawks make. The cuddly promise of otters?
Don't believe it. A pause in grooming and the sea has them
by the skin in an icy grip. Evolution screams their time is past,
and they chain themselves to kelp at night to keep from floating away.
The ocean swallows them whole.

I grew up in Illinois, a place that seemed to need me
or at least lay down readily beneath my feet.
To come to this sea—never has a place needed me less,
the rising expanse and its patches of vegetation
amplifying the loneliness, roiling the longing
into the storms that never seem to come.

Like so many I thought I'd stride into the warm embrace of California.
When the fog lipped Silicon Valley's scenic frame of hills
and shrouded the sky, I wondered how far I'd have to ride
to find the source of that vision, to learn the language.
You want visions? Ha! Here's a language carved, craven.

The monks dug into the side of Big Sur choose silence
and bread, prayers, and psalms scribed and transcribed,
petroglyphs left by the wind that say: KEEP OFF.
The keeper of the Zen monastery down the road unwinds
his Mercedes up the hill. He is not long for this world.

Look but don't touch. Take nothing away.

The sea has worn holes in the stones, and the seals
at Año Nuevo hoist themselves onto a shabby velvet couch
in an abandoned coast station. Can you hear them bark,
playing King of the Mountain? Can you imagine that throne?
Keep your oars close to the body. Those seals
could take a bite right out of your hide.

NOT THIS

Better aliens had come and taken you,
Better relocated in the witness protection program,
Better transferred to the Arctic Circle, to Timbuktu,
Better awaken somewhere not knowing
Who or where you are and pick up from there,
Better separated at birth into adoption,
Better even a truck swerved onto the shoulder
Where you bent changing a tire and I lost you
Through no fault of my own, better that wild grief,
Better there were no God or Heaven or Hell,
Better to wake up a cockroach with an apple in my back
Knowing once I was that person and had that other life,
Better to live without work, without music,
Without books, than without you,
On gruel and water, better the desert island.
Better, much better, to lose my arm, my sight,
My hearing, than to hear you say
You never loved me, I never loved you.

THE ICE MAN

One must have a mind of winter
                        Wallace Stevens

He is there in December, early,
as soon as the ice will hold a deer or a man
but not a truck. He is there sitting on an overturned bucket,
his auger beside him. There he is, solitary, motionless,
and slightly ridiculous in the late afternoon
when the sky is already pink, the low temperature dropping,
or when the sky is gray. He faces away from the road.
Sometimes he sees only gray shore and gray sky and gray surface.
Sometimes the only mark is the hole he drilled, his line.

SYNOPSIS

Act 1

Interior of John Gordon's mansion.

Bob and Dick—Gordon's two shiftless sons.

Gordon's fruitless efforts to make men of them.

His socially ambitious wife.

Their daughter Margaret.

The mysterious Countess Du Prey.

The visit of Betty Green.

Act 2

The curse of wealth.

A father's love for his children.

The love of Betty Green.

Betty makes a proposition.

Bob and Dick accept.

Bob accepts Gordon's offer.

A villain's treachery.

The ruin of Gordon.

Act 3

Gordon's illness.

The downfall of Dick.

A secret in John Gordon's life.

Bob learns the truth.

Gordon's trust in Bob.

Bob makes a solemn promise.

The death of Gordon.

44

Act 4
Dick's mistake.
Bob's loyalty.
Van Darcy threatens.
Countess Du Prey turns the tables.
Betty's decision.
Dick acknowledges his guilt.
Bob's secret becomes known.
A happy ending.

DISSOLUTION

I withdrew my money
with a single signature.
The woman at the bank was friendly
and pretended not to know
what was going on. Nothing personal.

Two weeks shy of five official years,
with no kids and no major assets or debt,
the State of California required
nothing but that I take the paper
from the hand of the clerk at my door.
They call it Dissolution of Marriage.

The man was called a server.
He smiled. He had advised.
Money had changed hands,
but it did not cost me a dime.

One or both of us were free
or without recourse
or just counting the months
until we could begin again.

TO BEGIN AGAIN

for F.H.

I look for your face in the pictures
of your children, and for that other face,
their mother's. She must have brown eyes,

this woman, the ex. No matter how
we try to X them out, replacing their names
with that one generic syllable,

they are still with us. We still possess
them, mine and yours. I touch your hand
to my belly as to a scar—that's him, there,

how vulnerable I feel to be touched
with the old worry about any new body
and something else he left behind.

I want to use the words of war wounds,
shrapnel, because it feels like a hunk
of molten lead has pierced me, the scar not neat,

though the only mark on me is the way
my eyelids register the experience.
I want to erase that look, but it has become me

like those children you keep giving away
a few hours each week so we can meet
each other, as free as we are able to be.

IN PRAISE OF THE YAK

Mr. Hooper quit the yak business
and went back to Christmas trees
after the goring, right through his gut.
Like any good farmer he did not blame the animal.
Lost sight of the babes for a moment, and then—
For months afterward he rode his golf cart
while the hole through his center healed up.
He was lucky to be alive, lucky indeed.

Now all that's left of the herd—
the beasts, pasture, electric fence—
is this heap of compost dumped
for the benefit of my garden.
Each year I unearth a clavicle, vertebrae,
sometimes a tibia or fibia,
and hunks of hide bound in burnt fur.
I excavate my dig and rejoice.

Yaks are lean and nutritious,
farmer-friendly, easy calvers,
cousin to the American bison!
They survive the coldest winters
and require very little shelter.
Mountain cow, grunting ox, coyote scarecrow,
fed on one third the pasture of cows.
Their small hooves aerate the soil.

Yak meat is mild in flavor, a clean finish on the palate.
Yak meat is prized for its many health benefits.

How hot must that pile of dung have been
to burn up an entire yak? More than one.
Every spring I sink my shovel into it
and marvel at its richness and fine quality,
perfect for the potatoes, well draining,
nourishing the roots. Premium organic matter.

Then I leave it, the shaggy pile, giant chia pet
that will sprout a coat of weeds in a week.
Next spring I'll gore that hide again
and continue to grow food and live off the beast.

THREE POEMS ON THE BIRTH
OF SAINT JOHN THE BAPTIST

ZECHARIAH

Because I spoke too quickly, I was left speechless.
Didn't Abraham also ask the Lord to prove himself?
He paid the price at the altars of sacrifice.

The cinder was pressed to my lips and I was silent,
the incense my anointing. And when I emerged
from the holy of holies, everyone saw the Glory of God,

whose name I dare not speak, the one my son would proclaim.

ARCHANGEL GABRIEL

With water to make clean John will come.

With a spirit of fire he will come.

When he comes the people will know him.

He will breathe words of fire on them and they will go down into death for
the Lord.

His hand will lead them beneath the water and they will rise with new
hearts for the Lord.

The world will know fire and water from his hand.

The world will know fire and water from his mouth.

They will say of him: "He eats locusts and wild honey, he is a man of dust, a
product of mud and clay."

He does not drink wine but he is wilder than any drunk or madman.

When we look at him we see the earth.

When he speaks we hear God. His word is fire, his word is water, his word is
the future and the past.

Surely this man is of fire and water.

When we listen to him we hear the Son of God.

He proclaims God to us, this man, John.

ELIZABETH

Like Sarah, mother of promise, I was barren.
Perhaps God would do for me what he did for her.
This was my hope, my prayer.

What could I do but be faithful, a daughter of Aaron?
Servants of Abraham and Moses, we have our parts.
Like Sarah, mother of promise, I was barren.

The Spirit of God prepared me to receive,
and the herald grew in my womb.
This was my hope, my prayer, speaking

for the baby who leapt in greeting:
Blessed are you, and blessed the fruit of your womb.
Like Sarah, I was a mother of promise.

How could we know what was to come?
We had life inside us, and that was all
the rejoicing, hope, and prayer we could contain.

They came to bring life to the world,
to turn children to parents, parents to God.
Like Sarah, we were bearing promised sons.
This was my hope, my prayer.

I GREET THE FALL

for Paula

After two years of so much loss
it had the shape of a country song—
my car crashed, my husband and my cat
run away, my job, my home put in storage,
the friends that fell silent or chose sides,
the in-laws and an in-law's child taken
by the State and no words to sing it—
God would have had to start carving
from my body itself to take more.

Some days I'd start to speak and lose my breath.

I left the sad crowded shore of California
and moved to a place where the leaves fall.

And the leaves fell slowly to the earth,
spinning and floating in twos and threes
down to the still surface of the lake.
Overnight they dropped and blew around
until they covered all the ground.

It did not feel like loss at all.

The birch trunks were such a glory,
the gnarled branches of an oak by the water,
the two maples still themselves
without their party dresses on.

Someone built a fire one night in my yard
and I saw a shooting star, even that.
The frost formed like white moss
and I found myself not alone
in singing and celebration.

INSTRUCTIONS FOR THE SECOND WIFE

When you move into his house, where none of the colors can be changed, and the furniture all fits just so in the spaces, and the paintings are already sized to the walls, and you know that though it is very, very nice, it is not something you yourself ever would have chosen, begin by cleaning. Clean well and deep. Empty the spaces room by room, clean into the corners, and add something of your own to what you put back. Try not to hold onto categories like "my laundry basket, his laundry basket."

His work clothes might be too dirty after days in the field to mix with your own. That's okay. Do your own laundry still, slipping something dark down the chute now and then, a black shirt, some underwear, socks, jeans, until all the pieces mingle. It takes time.

To claim the house, paint the outside. He'll thank you and say it isn't necessary, a task left over from before you signed on, but it is necessary. Do it. Climb the ladder to the second floor. Get some paint on the windowsill. Paint carefully around the vents. Soak up the spaces and the hidden nooks. Learn how many difficult eaves and crannies there are to it. See how the cement was painted before and so must be painted this time too, up to the first row of shakes.

You'll spend a lot of time looking for things. That's normal. Have one place where you can tell him—if you want to move something of mine, or want it put away, put it here, on this desk, this table, this shelf, this step.

Begin by cooking. Get to know the oven and which burners burn hottest and fastest. How to pull out the bowls you need and how to slide them back into place. Looking for a pot you'll discover another drawer with odds and ends you can remove, old birthday hats or children's party plates. You can put the picnic plates there, the plastic cups. Make ordinary dishes and difficult dishes, ones you thought you'd never make again, with expensive cheese sauces and crusts.

Be the one who brings in the tomatoes and beans and squash, even if you weren't the one who planted them. Blanch and peel them and freeze them in bags for stews. You'll be ready for winter. You'll be ready next year. Make a list of what you want to grow, things you miss. Things you've never planted.

Get a book on vegetable gardening, or find one in the basement on a shelf. When the vines have died, take them down, work the soil, add compost, mulch. Bring a few flowers inside, ones that won't winter over. Decide which bulbs you don't like and dig them out before they can emerge again. Leave room for herbs below the kitchen window. Plant perennials from your mother's garden. Learn to do things you haven't ever done before, things that will make you belong to this place.

MINNESOTA SONNET

That time of year it is when leaves have turned
and lost their grip on limbs, blown down
an inch deep and brown, covering the bones
of kindling, hidden paths, the season's varied dead.
The waters set in spiking weeds assert
their true nature as precious stones, amber and jade,
bidding the deer approach for one more drink
before the ice encroaches. Everywhere
the acorn stores of busy, slender, panicked squirrels.
Could this really be winter coming on,
with the sun this bright at noon, the sky this blue?
See what happens in the slant of five o'clock.
The trees, stripped naked, reveal their strength;
the wind bares its teeth and the lake shivers.

MINDFULNESS IN MID-NOVEMBER

The Thich Nhat Hanh group is on retreat.
A sign on the bathroom mirror says: "Be free here."
A sign by the door says: "You have arrived."
There is a poem about drinking tea by the boxes of tea.

The participants walk silently in the woods.
People place large sticks by the door
intentionally. Their beauty arrests me.
Their purpose eludes me.

I am working: bills, mailing lists,
but every twenty minutes the timer
(my coat smothering its *tick, tick, tick*)
rings and I rise and go out to move the hose.

Mid-November. It has been bitter cold
and I need to water the last of thirty-five new trees.
Today the temperature is up to fifty degrees.
It is the last chance. I am almost too late.

A woman sits on a bench with her face to the sun.
I walk the long drive, past the metal birdbath
with its skin of ice, past the row of Priuses
with their bumper stickers promoting peace.

Late this morning I lifted the hose
and bent it, cracking the ice inside.
Water squirted from the spigot, under pressure,
until a trickle melted the long, long line.

Now water flows freely and I count down
my charges: *nine, eight, seven . . .*
I haul the long hose back around
to stretch out to the final grove.

The woman comes close to stare at the kinks
as the hose loops and I hope she'll help
if it catches on a root. I don't think she will.
It is a labor. It is a chore. It is my job.

The trees drink deeply for ten minutes,
then the water fills their bowl of earth.
I think I'll skip a small tree.
It's Friday. I want to get home.

But then I don't want to go home.
I don't want to be anywhere but here,
watering the trees, startled by the timer
and rising from my chair. Going out.

The changing light doesn't panic me.
The day is merely passing over.
I stand on the precipice of winter,
moving the hose into the bowl of the last tree.

Outside, the silent group has gathered.
With their sticks they process next door.
They spread out in the baseball diamond,
facing the dying light, perfectly still.

Then collectively they move
like warriors, scooping the earth,
lifting the sky, balancing the world
on an axis, between hello and goodbye.

RETURN OF THE SANDHILL CRANES

At the close of this and every long winter
when the length of the day
and height of the sun say more
than the still-frozen ground,

we hope you will return to us,
find the small patch in the wetland
shining like a hand mirror,
the particular reed-pocked marsh
just south of our house.

And then, during a March snowstorm
as I am planting pepper seeds
in a hive of pots on the windowsill
with heat to trick them awake,
you announce your arrival
with rolling chortles and raspy trumpeting.

And a few mornings later you are heard
protesting the Canada geese who pause here,
asserting your ownership of this particular spot.
I see you, sentinels flanking the water,
and hear your vulgar cries:
No room! Push off! Move on!

What coordinates get you exactly here,
how related to the hours, the slant of the sun,
wind resistance? Do you look for the house,
for the oak, hear the ping of some black box?

We hear bad news while you're away:
oil spills, changing winds and currents,
encroachments on the migration routes,
so we worry. What if you're blown off course,
diverted, misdirected, or just plain killed?

Today the geese pass overhead
in long loud honking vees and ragged lines.
They shout from the back of the flock:
How much farther? and *Are we there yet?*

You are off-site, running the errands
of return, getting resettled and restocked.
I know you're not far, and the geese
seem to have gotten the message, too.

Even though the frost still holds the ground
and my pitchfork stops halfway into the bed,
I begin my annual conversation with the land.
But you wake the earth, you great birds,
your gawky grandeur, your masked heads,
your calls bouncing off my window:
Awake! Awake! Awake! Again! Again! Again!

MY TWO HUSBANDS

My husband went into nature, first the north woods of Michigan,
then the Sierras, the Pacific Coast Trail, whatever wildness he could find,
and spent his nights in poetry, Jeffers and Rexroth and Snyder,
thinking about wilderness and ideas of wilderness.
He was a Romantic—free and open-hearted,
happiest naked or nearly so, filtering the water
from an alpine pond, smelling the Jeffrey pines
and pronouncing them vanilla, building camp.
I followed him down the trail and admired
the way his legs moved, how his pack sat on his hips,
how he blew a fire to life with his bellows breath.
He told me about Emerson and Thoreau and Wendell Berry.

My husband studied theology, bought a parcel of land
from the monastery, and while teaching religion,
learned how to make a prairie, and cultivated.
He bought machinery and built a shed to house it.
He is a man of Virtue—duty-bound and open-hearted,
happiest working outside, pulling weeds or mowing paths.
I followed him into the garden, where he built me twelve raised beds,
snaking hoses and planting straight rows, chopping weeds with my hoe.
I love to see him covered in dirt, his broad-brimmed hat,
his easy amble on the path he's worn between his shop and our house.
In the evening we sit down over a plate of good food and talk
about the news of the day, the frustrations of working the land, the triumphs,
the breezes cooling us through the screen of the porch.
He told me about Hauerwas and McIntyre and Wendell Berry.

My husbands wake up early and make coffee,
one twelve cups in a percolator, the other espresso in a demitasse.
One filled the house with books of poetry, the other with furniture
that is sleek and modern, made of wood and metal.
One put the bed on wheels, so we can roll it to the window and hear the frogs,
while the other prefers no shelter at all, a bedroll on the ground.
Each night both men go outside and smoke a single cigarette. I think it is just
because they long to see the stars and think about the rightness of the world.

EATING THE GARDEN

We began with arugula and other delicate leaves
that went limp when we washed them, grown on the windowsill.
In the cold frame the young greens stayed young
and the spinach froze, and we brushed off the snow into May.
Then with one day's sudden warmth, the spinach bolted.
We cut the emerging asparagus stalks at their cold roots.
We pulled up rhubarb and made bars, then made jam.
We pulled too soon the wispy parsnips, pale from winter sleep,
to make room for chard and carrots and the kale that is with us still.
We ate radishes, fried in a pan, with their greens.
We ate the peas in their pods, peas snapped, peas shelled.
We ate the curly lettuce, the tender lettuce, and the romaine heads.
We ate the beets and their greens (greens, always greens).
We roasted and sliced and pureed the beets into bright pink pesto.
We wondered what comes next, tired of greens.
We hungered for cucumbers and watched the bees in the blossoms.
We made dressings, bought fancy vinegar, bought buttermilk.
We ate carrots, then, and broccoli. We ate beans.
The onions lay down and the garlic ripened, and we dried them on an old bed frame
and tucked them into burlap-lined laundry baskets in the basement.
We filled a Royal Basmati Rice sack with garlic heads and zipped it closed.
Then, finally, we ate the cucumbers and summer squash.
We searched for it under giant leaves, caught it small, grilled and sliced.
We reached through the trellis for the prickly cukes. We pickled with the copious dill.
We protected the snow-white heads of cauliflower from the sun with their own leaves.
We harvested the precious few, grown large and meaty, and had a feast.
Then we ate cherry tomatoes, grilled and raw, popped in our mouths,
with basil and oil and vinegar, alongside every dish. We made salsa,
and the tomatillos came, and we made sauce and jam and salsa some more,

and the full-grown tomatoes, and we sliced them on sandwiches
and stuffed them into jars for winter stews, and made sauce.
We made pesto and froze it in ice cube trays, then bags.
And peppers!
We dug potatoes by the bucketful and beans and more beans.
We planted more beets, then, and turnips, and greens.
They languished in the late heat and drought, but quickly grew.
We bought corn from the farmer and cut it from the cob for winter.
We ate it by the dozen, even though we had too many vegetables to eat.
We shelled dry beans and cooked the not-so-dry beans and ate them.
We cut the Brussels sprouts from the stalks and ate them.
We were glad we didn't plant cabbage, even as we scanned ads for sauerkraut crocks.
We made pepper sauce and our favorite Indian dishes, with tomatoes and peppers
        and spice.
We made tomato soup and pepper soup and stuffed the peppers with cheese.
We strung the paprika for drying and grinding. We froze the poblanos.
We ate the watermelon, almost too late, heavy and sweet.
We were disappointed by the winter squash, even as it filled our baskets:
butternut, acorn, pumpkin, delicata. We prepared to roast. And roast and roast.
We dreamed of soup, of pies, of stews. We filled the pantry shelves with jars.
We took down the trellises. We picked our peck of apples.
We pulled up the leeks, narrow but deep, and prized them, and made them last,
        and everything made with them was good.
As usual, we ignored the kale and chard, and then we were grateful for it.
We heard the first shots of pheasant season, then deer.
We saw the cranes make their last flight over our heads, north to south.
We planted the garlic cloves and heaped their beds with straw.
We dug in compost and stored the cages and hoses and stakes.
All along we gave away, grateful, and wishing there was more.

THE TRUCK

I watch my husband crouch behind his truck. He's shooting the breeze with his mechanic and hasn't seen me pull up. He hops onto the trailer and I enjoy watching him, his ease, his length, as he leans back in his dark, long-sleeved t-shirt and work pants, a thin moon of white at the collar. After he glances back at the road a second time, the mechanic asks him what he's looking for.

He says, *My wife. She's coming to pick me up.*

Is that her? The mechanic asks, pointing.

My husband sees me then and stands, smiling broadly. He expects me to be impatient, as I so often am on these rescue missions when the truck has stranded him again. But I've fully relaxed into his happiness, this former teacher who loves the broken-down truck and every glorious outdoor day, and his wife come to pick him up.

ACKNOWLEDGMENTS

The author gratefully acknowledges The David and Julia White Foundation, The Anderson Center, the Collegeville Institute for Ecumenical and Cultural Research, The Virginia Center for the Creative Arts, and The MacDowell Colony for gifts of space and support while many of these poems were written.

The following poems and lyric prose appeared previously in publications:

"Song for a Green Season," *Spoon River Poetry Review*.

"To Begin Again," "Precious Things," and "A Girl," *Great River Review*.

"Pacific," *Eclipse*.

"December, January, February," *Spirituality & Health*.

"Meditation for a Century Just Begun," *Crab Orchard Review*.

"After Vespers, Saturday," *Red Rock Review*.

"Atlantic," and "Mount Rainier," *Interdisciplinary Studies in Literature and Environment*.

"Not This," *Schuylkill Valley Journal of the Arts*.

"Three Poems on the Birth of Saint John the Baptist" were commissioned for the sesquicentennial celebration of Saint John's Abbey in Collegeville, Minnesota, and proclaimed in the Abbey Church on the Vigil of the Feast of Saint John the Baptist, June 23, 2006.

NOTES

HIGH PLACES The book referred to by this poem is *Hinds Feet on High Places*, a Christian classic by Hannah Hurnard.

AFTER *THE ENTRY OF CHRIST INTO CHICAGO IN 1976* by Roger Brown: I.C. is an abbreviation for the Illinois Central railroad line. The painting is in the collection of the Museum of Contemporary Art Chicago.

SYNOPSIS This is a found poem taken from the play *Gilded Youth*, written by my husband's grandfather Martin J. Heymans. It is a morality play/melodrama published in 1926 by the Catholic Dramatic Movement of Briggsville, Wisconsin, whose purpose was "to provide and support clean and wholesome stage productions in order to make the Catholic stage again what it was and what it should be, a place of decent entertainment, an educational institution, a part of the great program of Catholic Action, the handmaid of religion." The movement also published "white lists of current clean plays" and distributed them free of charge.

I'LL TAKE YOU HOME AGAIN The public domain song "I'll Take You Home Again, Kathleen," was written in 1875 by German-American Thomas Paine Westendorf for his wife Jennie. It was written as a response to an Irish-American folk song popular at the time, "Barney, Take Me Home Again." Westendorf wrote and debuted the song where he worked at the time, a juvenile correctional facility in Plainfield, Indiana.

BRINGING THE BODY DOWN The German phrases in English are: *Alle sind tot . . . Aber wie?* All are dead . . . But how? *Vorsicht ist besser als Nachsicht.* Foresight is better than hindsight (idiomatically: Hindsight is 20/20).

AFTER VESPERS, SATURDAY Each week in a Benedictine monastery the assignments for kitchen duty and readers changes. This change is marked during a liturgy before sundown on Saturday, when a new liturgical week begins.